CLEOPATRA

· The Search for the Last Queen of Egypt ·

· Official Exhibition Guide ·

BECKON BOOKS

CLEOPATRA

Who Was Cleopatra?

Cleopatra VII, the last queen of Egypt, is one of the most celebrated figures in history. Fiercely intelligent as well as beautiful, she was descended from a Greek dynasty, the Ptolemies. She encouraged scholarship and learning, wrote books, and was the first Ptolemaic pharaoh to speak Egyptian as well as Greek. Cleopatra was anointed pharaoh at seventeen, co-ruling the powerful and prosperous land of Egypt with her younger brother and husband, Ptolemy XIII. When Ptolemy challenged her claim to the throne, Cleopatra used her charm and brilliance to win the favor of Julius Caesar and ensure her brother's defeat. In 44 B.C., Julius Caesar was assassinated. Cleopatra then forged a passionate alliance with Roman general and leader Mark Antony to battle Caesar's heir, Octavian. Their efforts, however, were doomed. Ultimately, Antony took his own life and Cleopatra was taken prisoner. In 30 B.C., with the help of her devoted servants, Cleopatra died by her own hand rather than face public humiliation in her enemy's streets.

STATUE OF A QUEEN Above and opposite: This black stone queen is distinguished by inlaid eyes, plaited hair, and thinly draped robes.

SITULA WITH GREEK INSCRIPTION Right: This bucket, or situla, has an inscription in Greek referring to the god Bacchus. Items such as these were often used for religious libations.

"[She] possessed a most charming voice and a knowledge of how to make herself agreeable to everyone."
— *Cassius Dio, Roman History, 202 A.D.*

UNDERWATER WORLD Various artifacts—including vessels and ancient sculptures—dot the sandy floor.

THE LOST QUEEN

Unearthing Cleopatra

For more than two thousand years, little was known of the queen of Egypt. The Romans tried to rewrite her history. And four centuries after her death, earthquakes and a tidal wave demolished her glorious city of Alexandria. Today, archaeologists Zahi Hawass and Franck Goddio have pieced together new evidence about her life. Underwater archaeologist Goddio has spent twenty years searching for traces of Cleopatra, mapping the entire port of ancient Alexandria and uncovering parts of her great palace. He has traced Cleopatra's journeys and discovered two lost cities that were instrumental to her reign: Canopus, a site of religious pilgrimage, and the strategic outpost of Heracleion. Dr. Zahi Hawass, Egypt's most senior archaeologist and secretary general of the Supreme Council of Antiquities, has found evidence at Taposiris Magna, near Alexandria, to suggest that Cleopatra's fabled tomb may be close by. Now, these clues have been brought together to reveal where Cleopatra lived, the places she knew, and the objects she may have touched.

ZAHI HAWASS Above: Renowned Egyptian archaeologist Dr. Zahi Hawass on site at Taposiris Magna, where he believes Cleopatra is buried.

FRANCK GODDIO Above: French underwater archaeologist Franck Goddio has spent more than two decades unearthing portions of Cleopatra's world.

OSIRIS-CANOPUS JAR Franck Goddio holds this sacred Osiris-Canopus jar the same way a priest would have carried it two thousand years ago.

The Line of the PTOLEMIES

PTOLEMY I Soter
CA 367–283 B.C., R. 304–283 B.C.

PTOLEMY II Philadelphus
309–246 B.C., R. 283–245 B.C.

ARSINOË II
316–270 B.C.

PTOLEMY III Euergetes
282–221 B.C., R. 246–222 B.C.

PTOLEMY IV Philopator
238–205 B.C., R. 221–205 B.C.

ARSINOË III
245–204 B.C.

PTOLEMY V Epiphanes
210–180 B.C., R. 205–180 B.C.

PTOLEMY VI Philomaetor
186–145 B.C., R. 181–145 B.C.

CLEOPATRA II
185–116 B.C.

PTOLEMY VIII Physcon Euergetes II
182–116 B.C., R. 170–116 B.C.

PTOLEMY VII Neos Philopator
CA 150–144 B.C., R. 145–144 B.C.

CLEOPATRA III
161–101 B.C., R. 142–101 B.C.

PTOLEMY IX Lathyrus, Soter II
CA 140–81 B.C., R. 116–110 B.C.
109–107 B.C., 88–80 B.C.

CLEOPATRA IV
CA 140–112 B.C., R. 116–115 B.C.

PTOLEMY X Alexander I
CA 140–88 B.C., R. 110–109 B.C., 107–88 B.C.

PTOLEMY XI Alexander II
CA 105–80 B.C., R. 80 B.C.

CLEOPATRA V Selene
140–69 B.C., R. 131–69 B.C.

CLEOPATRA-BERENICE III
238–205 B.C., R. 221–205 B.C.

PTOLEMY XII Neos Dionysus
117–51 B.C., R. 80–58 B.C., 55–51 B.C.

CLEOPATRA VI Tryphaena
75–57 B.C., R. 58–57 B.C.

BERENICE IV
77–55 B.C., R. 57–55 B.C.

CLEOPATRA VII Philopator
69–30 B.C., R. 51–49 B.C., 48–30 B.C.

ARSINOE IV
CA 67–41 B.C., R. 48–46 B.C.

PTOLEMY XIII
62–47 B.C., R. 51–47 B.C.

PTOLEMY XIV
CA 60–44 B.C., R. 47–44 B.C.

PTOLEMY XV Caesarion
47–30 B.C., R. 44–30 B.C.

ALEXANDER Helios
40–CA 27 B.C.

CLEOPATRA Selene
40 B.C.–CA 6 A.D.

PTOLEMY Philadelphus
36–29 B.C.

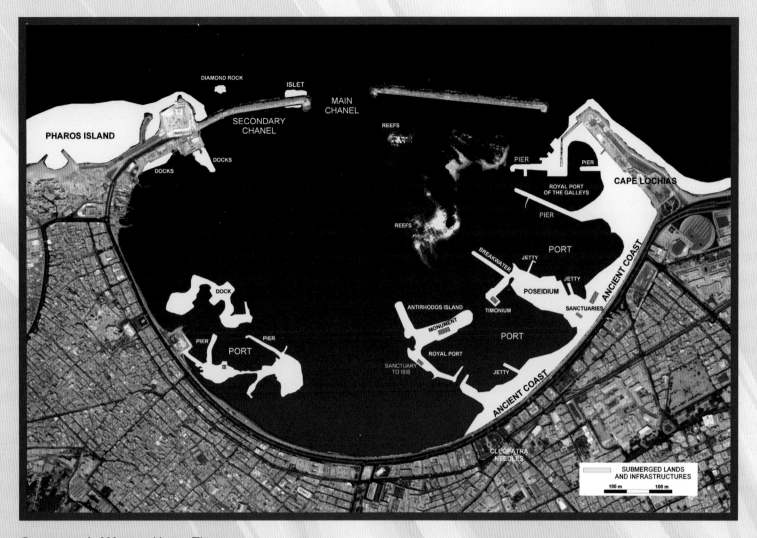

Above: The following labels appear on the map: DIAMOND ROCK, ISLET, MAIN CHANEL, PHAROS ISLAND, SECONDARY CHANEL, REEFS, PIER, PIER, DOCKS, DOCKS, ROYAL PORT OF THE GALLEYS, CAPE LOCHIAS, REEFS, PIER, PORT, BREAKWATER, JETTY, JETTY, DOCK, POSEIDIUM, ANTIRHODOS ISLAND, TIMONIUM, SANCTUARIES, ANCIENT COAST, PIER, PORT, MONUMENT, PORT, PIER, SANCTUARY TO ISIS, ROYAL PORT, JETTY, ANCIENT COAST, CLEOPATRA NEEDLES, SUBMERGED LANDS AND INFRASTRUCTURES, 100 m, 100 m

CLEOPATRA'S WORLD Above: This map of the Bay of Alexandria shows one of the sites surveyed by Franck Goddio's team. The team's goal was to explore three specific sites: the great port of Alexandria and two areas in Aboukir, which had disappeared under the sea due to natural catastrophes.

LINE OF THE PTOLEMIES Opposite: Cleopatra descended from the Ptolemies, who ruled Egypt beginning in 304 B.C. The first pharaoh in the line, Ptolemy I, had been a general under Alexander the Great. The dynasty ended with Cleopatra's death in 30 B.C.

"*At every dive carried out by members of the team, the veil of mystery over these lost cities of Egypt was lifted a little further. Gradually, sixteen centuries of a history among the richest in the Mediterranean world were revealed.*"

— *Franck Goddio*

BLACK STONE QUEEN A black stone queen buried in the sand stares through the waters of Canopus.

CANOPUS

City of Sin, City of God

Cleopatra came to the city of Canopus to pray and play. Canopus—a short boat ride from Alexandria—was known throughout the ancient world as a place to relax and have fun. But Canopus was also a religious center. The city's main shrine, dedicated to the god Sarapis, drew thousands of pilgrims in search of cures for all kinds of ailments. They came from across the Mediterranean and spent the night sleeping outside Sarapis's temple, the Sarapeum. The cures they sought were revealed in dreams the priest would interpret the following morning. Sarapis was a combination of gods, including Dionysus, the Greek god of wine. His devotees released their cares and worries in wild celebrations. Sarapis also took on the functions of Osiris, the ancient Egyptian god of the afterlife. Osiris's annual death and rebirth promised eternal life and ensured fertile lands for Egypt. With his reputation for performing miracles, Sarapis was very popular. Many cities had their own Sarapeum, but the one at Canopus was famed throughout the region.

NAOS OF THE DECADES Above: This naos—an inner shrine that held the temple god—may be the world's first astrological chart. The year was divided into thirty-six decades, or ten-day periods. Each followed the movement of a star called a decans, which was thought to guide earthly events.

HEAD OF A PHARAOH Left: Egyptian pharaohs, such as the one represented by this statue head, married their siblings. Their children became their uncontested heirs and automatically inherited the Egyptian throne.

GALLERY OF CANOPUS The ancient Canopic region, near the modern city of Alexandria, had been submerged for centuries and was believed to be lost to legend when Franck Goddio's team began its exploration. The most significant discoveries here include the location of the famous temple of Sarapis and the missing pieces of the Naos of the Decades.

they confirmed that this was indeed Sarapis.

Portrait of
a Pharaoh

CANOPUS

EAST CANOPUS

Naos of the Decades

STATUETTES OF ISIS AND OSIRIS The ancient Egyptians revered the gods Isis (left) and Osiris (right). Cleopatra and her Ptolemaic ancestors maintained control of the country by honoring the Egyptian gods and adapting them for their own political needs.

STATUETTE OF HARPOKRATES Far left: Harpokrates was the young son of Isis and Osiris. Before the Greeks transformed him into a boy-god, he was depicted with a falcon head as the god Horus.

STATUETTE OF OSIRIS AND VOTIVE BOAT Left and below: During the annual procession of Osiris, participants left figures of Osiris and boats as votives.

NAOS OF THE DECADES Opposite: Shown is the reverse side of the Naos of the Decades. Early Christians smashed the naos to pieces. The top section was found on land in 1776, and it entered the Louvre in Paris in 1817. In 1940, the lower and rear walls were discovered on the seashore of the Bay of Aboukir. Franck Goddio found the remaining pieces in the Bay of Aboukir in 1999.

HEAD OF SARAPIS Below: This head of the god Sarapis, found on the ocean floor of Canopus, can be dated to around the second century B.C.

THE LIFE OF CLEOPATRA

In accordance with Ptolemaic traditions, on the very day that Cleopatra was crowned Pharaoh of Egypt, she also became the divine goddess Isis, the sister and wife of Osiris. Isis was revered as Osiris's wife and sister, and was an important goddess in her own right. Cleopatra's close identification with the god strengthened her hold on the Egyptian throne and increased her allure outside the kingdom. As Isis, Cleopatra took part in libation rites at the temple of the Sarapeum—dedicated to the god Sarapis—using religious instruments to pour offerings of wine, honey, milk, oil, juice, or other liquids. Apart from the priest, the only person allowed to enter the temple was the pharaoh. The Sarapeum at Canopus provided an important sanctuary for Cleopatra and earlier Ptolemaic pharaohs, who offered the deity statues in their own likeness.

Sarah Bernhardt (1844–1923) in the Role of Cleopatra by Georges Jules Victor Clairin, 1886.

"Cleopatra, indeed . . . when she appeared in public, assumed a robe sacred to Isis, and was addressed as the New Isis."
— Plutarch, Life of Antony, 110–15 A.D.

PTOLEMAIC KING AND QUEEN The most significant finds at Heracleion are these two colossal figures: a newly crowned Ptolemaic king and his queen, which stood guard before the ancient temple of Amun-*gereb*.

HERACLEION
Center of Religion, Gateway to Egypt

An ancient site of Mediterranean trade, Heracleion played host to Greek traders for centuries. This commercial center was linked to other towns in the region and far into Egypt through an intricate network of canals that led to the Nile. Heracleion was a crucial religious site, too. The Ptolemies journeyed there to the ancient temple of Amun-*gereb* to be granted the right to rule Egypt.

Every year, to guarantee the floods, the Ptolemies also traveled around Heracleion in a procession of boats to celebrate the god Osiris. On this journey, Cleopatra—the goddess Isis incarnate—accompanied the priest of Osiris as the boat sailed from east to west. Today, Heracleion lies submerged in the Bay of Aboukir, about seven miles from the coastline.

STATUE OF HAPY Above: A member of Franck Goddio's underwater team shines a light on a statue of the god Hapy.

THE HEM-HEM CROWN Right: Khonsu, god of the moon, was often shown wearing the hem-hem crown. The crown was a symbol of pharaonic power and authority, and was credited with magical abilities that would protect Egypt from any enemy.

"The entry of Osiris in the holy baroque takes place here yearly at the defined time, at the temple at [Heracleion]."
— The Canopus Decree, *circa* 239 B.C.

ANCIENT GODS Right: Statuettes of gods were central to Egyptian religious ceremonies. During these rituals, rich participants offered figures made of bronze and other metals, while the less wealthy clutched ceramic figures. Clockwise from top left: a falcon emblem depicting Horus, the son of Isis and Osiris; the head of Osiris, god of the dead and afterlife; the canine Anubis, ancient god of mummification and the journey into the afterlife; and the sacred bull of Memphis, called Apis by the Egyptians.

STATUETTE OF THE CAT BASTET Many ancient Egyptian gods were depicted with animal heads, like this cat-headed Bastet. Later, under the Ptolemies, the gods went through a transition, taking on human form in the tradition of Greek art.

HELMET For centuries, Egyptian rulers employed Greek mercenaries—who wore helmets like this—and positioned them at outposts throughout the Canopic region.

THE LIFE OF CLEOPATRA

After the assassination of Julius Caesar, Cleopatra and her Roman lover Mark Antony became entangled in a power struggle with Octavian, Caesar's heir. Although Caesar had a son by Cleopatra—named Caesarion—he never acknowledged the boy publicly. The political situation between Rome and Egypt had become tense and volatile, and Caesar knew Rome would never accept Caesarion as their leader. Instead, he had named his nephew Octavian as his successor. Cleopatra believed it was crucial to defeat Octavian, both for the future of her son and for the future of Egypt. Antony and Cleopatra amassed a fleet of ships and faced Octavian at the Battle of Actium. But Octavian hemmed them in, and Cleopatra was defeated.

Cleopatra Showing Octavius the Bust of Julius Caesar by **Pompeo Girolamo Batoni, 1700s.**

STATUETTE OF SEKHMET Far left: Sekhmet, the powerful warrior goddess of Upper Egypt, was depicted as a lioness.

STATUETTE OF ATHENA Left: The Greek goddess Athena was associated with the Egyptian goddess of wisdom, Neith, indicating the strong influence Greek mythology had on Egyptian religion and practices.

PHIALE Above: Cleopatra herself may have poured libations to the god Khonsu using this gold phiale recovered from underwater Heracleion. Traditionally, wine from a jug was poured into the phiale, which was then tipped to allow the wine to spill onto the ground.

STATUETTE OF KHONSU WITH LUNAR DISK Far right: Atop this figurine of the Egyptian child-god Khonsu sits a lunar disk, illuminating his path. Khonsu's temple in Heracleion was situated near the temple of Amon.

HEAD OF THE VULTURE-GODDESS NEKHBET Right: In early dynastic times, Nekhbet, goddess of Upper Egypt, was shown as a vulture. Later, Nekhbet became associated with other Egyptian goddesses such as Sekhmet.

STATUE OF HAPY Franck Goddio admires a massive figure of Hapy, god of the flooding of the Nile.

SPHINX The Ptolemies frequently placed sphinxes in front of temples throughout the Canopic region. With a human head and the body of a lion, the sphinx signified the intellectual capacity and physical power of a pharaoh.

ALEXANDRIA

Capital of the Ancient World

Cleopatra's grand palace sat on Antirhodos Island in the famous Portus Magnus—the great port of Alexandria. The city was founded by Alexander the Great shortly after he conquered Egypt in 332 B.C. Alexander had scoured the Mediterranean coast, looking for a seaport that would open Egypt up to the contemporary world. Alexandria was the perfect spot: close to the Nile delta and sheltered by a curved coastline that formed a natural barricade and offered a deep harbor. Alexandria became a commercial hub and a cultural center, the richest, most renowned, and most cosmopolitan metropolis of the ancient world. It was also a great intellectual center, its Great Library of Alexandria attracting scholars from around the world. With its white buildings, colonnades, and statues, the city looked Greek rather than Egyptian. In Cleopatra's day, the population of Alexandria was more than 500,000. Today, her island of Antirhodos is buried under the Alexandrian sea.

SPHINX Above: A diver examines a sphinx in the water where almost fifty experts have uncovered the remains of palaces, temples, and harbors.

COLOSSAL HEAD Left: This head is believed to represent Caesarion, the son of Cleopatra and Julius Caesar.

"On the streets of Aboukir and Alexandria, on the road along which the enormous statues of the king and queen were transported to the depot, the crowd applauded and cried out, 'Long live Ramses! Long live Cleopatra!'"

— Franck Goddio

Osiris Canopus

In the Canopic region, Osiris, god of the dead, was represented as a jar with a human head.

According to ancient legend, Osiris granted rebirth. He caused the sun to reappear every morning after its nightly journey through the underworld. It was only with his approval that a recently deceased pharaoh emerged as a god in the Afterlife.

A Ptolemaic king did not wait to die to become a god: once inaugurated as pharaoh, he became the earthly avatar of Osiris.

Auletes, the Flute Player

Sculpture description text

The city of Alexandria was thriving. But after years of indulgence, the Ptolemaic grasp on power was weakening. We learn though ancient sources of the deft political upheavals, maneuvering Egypt's independence, which culminating closer ties to Rome. Cleopatra, his favorite daughter, absorbed his diplomatic skills.

Colossal Head
Granodiorite
1st c. B.C.
ALEXANDRIA

Caesarion

Caesarion — little Caesar — was the son of Cleopatra and Julius Caesar. Cleopatra believed her son's future as a powerful leader was guaranteed by her alliance with Caesar, imperator of Rome. And she hoped that through Caesarion, whom this statue is believed to represent, Egypt would once again be restored to its ancient glory.

But Caesar never acknowledged Caesarion publicly. Instead, he named his nephew Octavian as his heir. On the death of Cleopatra's brother, Ptolemy XIV, the three-year-old Caesarion became Ptolemy XV, and ruled Egypt jointly with his mother.

GALLERY OF ALEXANDRIA The sphinxes, colossal head (most likely depicting Caesarion), and priest were found in the waters of Portus Magnus, the Port of Alexandria. The sphinx at far left resembles Cleopatra's father, King Ptolemy XII.

to touch the paveme

Cleopatra once w

— Franck Go

TEMPLE PRIEST This statue of a priest with a jar representing the god Osiris stood before the temple of Isis at Cleopatra's palace.

THE LIFE OF CLEOPATRA

Cleopatra's palace in Alexandria was decorated with vast quantities of gold, silver, and other precious metals. Its walls were covered in colorful friezes, its carved doors inlaid with tortoiseshell and glass and gems, and its pools stocked with lotus flowers and fish. There, the Egyptians celebrated the gods Dionysus, Osiris, and Sarapis by feasting on oysters, wild boar, baked fish and seafood, peacock and flamingo meat, roasted quail, and pastries that dripped with honey, figs, dates, and berries. They also served fine wines in gold goblets encrusted with jewels and had music and dancing. Outside Cleopatra's palace were lush gardens, and in the harbor, the magnificent Egyptian fleet stood guard. From Cleopatra's palace, she could look out on the famous Library of Alexandria, the most admired center of culture in the world. Mathematicians, philosophers, poets, and other scholars came there from all over to consult the library's many thousands of scrolls and to discuss ideas with their colleagues.

Death of Cleopatra **by Jacob Jordaens, 1653.**

OSIRIS-CANOPUS JAR Left: In the Canopic region, Osiris, god of the dead, was represented as a jar with a human head. Jars like this were used during rituals and ceremonies at the temple of Isis.

STONE WITH GOLD FRAGMENTS Below: The Ptolemies spent many hours feasting and carousing. As an expression of gratitude to the gods, they displayed their jewels and gold—as seen in this limestone receptacle—with great pride.

POWER AND BEAUTY

Fit for a Queue

Cleopatra was an intelligent, witty woman with considerable charisma who wooed and won two of the most powerful men of her day. Through her alliances with them, she maintained Egypt's independence. Yet though her beauty and charm were legendary, no one truly knows what Cleopatra looked like. After her death, the Roman emperor Octavian ordered all images of Cleopatra destroyed. Of the countless images created of the queen during her lifetime, only a handful of coins and sculptures remain. Few descriptions of Cleopatra exist from works written by Romans in the years after she died. Despite their dislike and disapproval of the last pharaoh, however, some grudgingly admitted that this powerful woman was a beauty.

ANCIENT NECKLACE Above: Cleopatra may have worn this type of double-chained necklace, made of gold and carnelian from the Greco-Roman period. (Courtesy of the Egyptian Museum, Cairo.)

STATUE OF ISIS Left: This black granite figure of Isis dates from Cleopatra's time. (Courtesy of the Egyptian Museum, Cairo.)

"Caesar was moved by the beauty of the damsel, which was enhanced by the fact that, being so fair, she seemed to have been wronged."
— *Florus*, Book II

STATUE OF A QUEEN The flawless body of this Ptolemaic queen in royal dress radiates beauty and dignity.

PAPYRUS DOCUMENT This papyrus document granted tax exemption from sales of imported wine to the Roman businessman Publius Canidius, a friend of Mark Antony. The manuscript was prepared by a court scribe. At the bottom, in a rare example of her handwriting, Cleopatra added the Greek word *ginesthoi*—meaning, "Make it happen." (Courtesy of the Egyptian Museum, Berlin.)

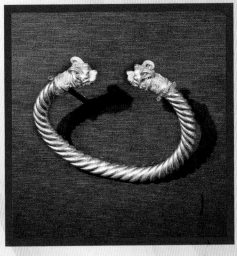

GOLD JEWELRY Above and left: Like her Ptolemaic ancestors, Cleopatra's lifestyle was opulent. She ate and drank from plates and goblets fashioned from the purest gold, draped her body with the finest silks and other rich fabrics, and adorned herself with magnificent jewelry—possibly with pieces similar to the ones shown here. (Courtesy of the Egyptian Museum, Cairo.)

BEAD IN THE SHAPE OF AN EYE OF HORUS Right: The god Horus was the falcon-headed son of Osiris and Isis. Necklaces with the Horus emblem—which signified health and well-being to Egyptians—were popular during Cleopatra's time.

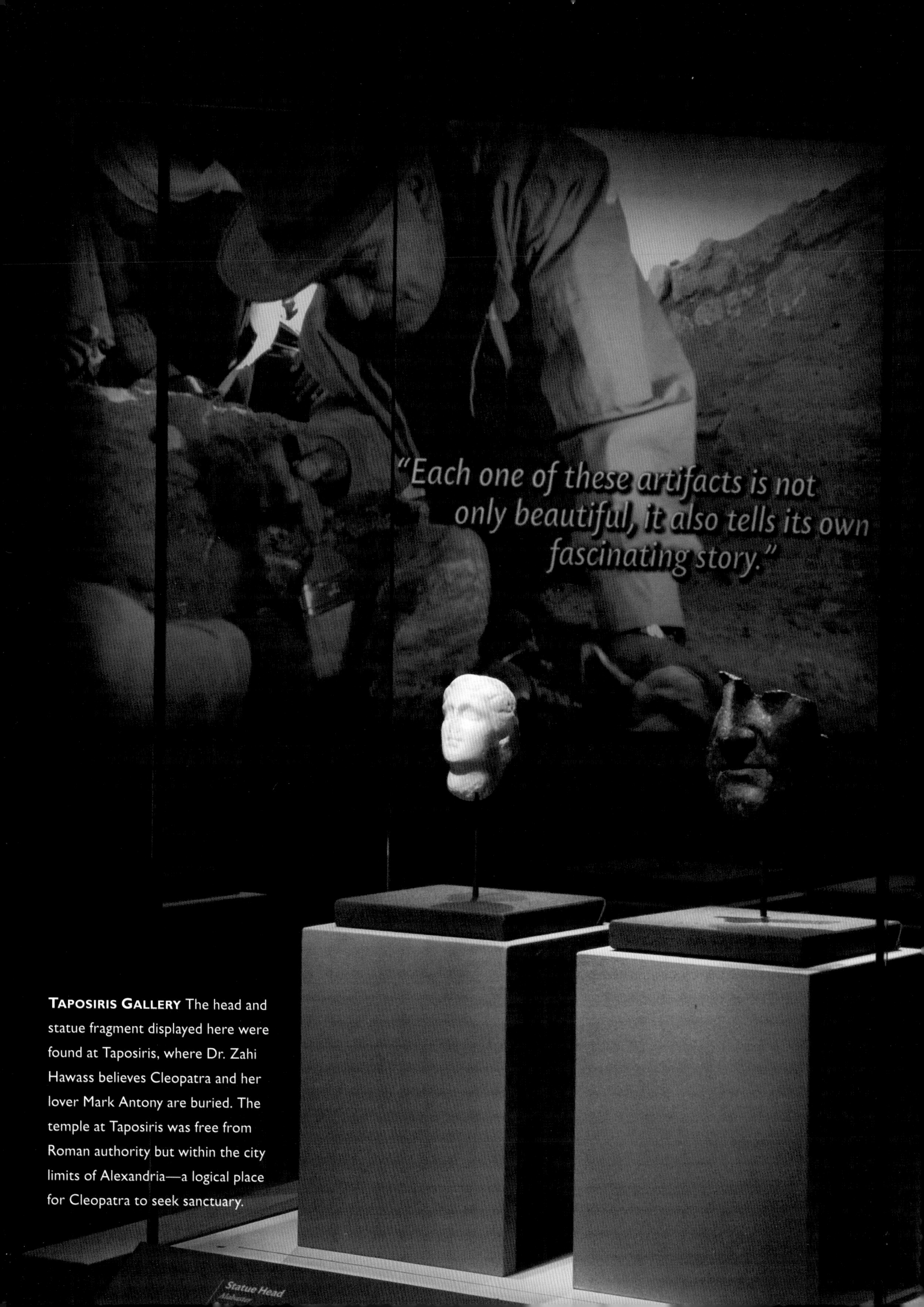

"Each one of these artifacts is not only beautiful, it also tells its own fascinating story."

TAPOSIRIS GALLERY The head and statue fragment displayed here were found at Taposiris, where Dr. Zahi Hawass believes Cleopatra and her lover Mark Antony are buried. The temple at Taposiris was free from Roman authority but within the city limits of Alexandria—a logical place for Cleopatra to seek sanctuary.

Statue Head
Alabaster

TAPOSIRIS
Search for the Tomb

For centuries, experts believed that Cleopatra and Mark Antony were buried in Alexandria, their tomb lost forever beneath the seabed. But recent historical evidence has challenged that idea. Cleopatra might not have wanted the Romans to destroy her remains. She may have instead placed her trust in the priests at the temple of Isis at Taposiris Magna, thirty miles along the coast from Alexandria, away from Roman control. Ptolemy II had founded the city of Taposiris, and Cleopatra knew the priests would protect her body with their lives. Now, Zahi Hawass and his team believe they are on the trail of Cleopatra's tomb. At a large cemetery uncovered near the temple and dated to the late Ptolemaic period, Hawass's team has found a number of mummies with golden masks as well as burial shafts that lead to tombs. Hawass is confident that the people buried there chose to locate their tombs near an important royal person. And he is certain that person is Cleopatra, the last queen of Egypt.

STATUE HEAD Above: Archaeologists believe this small alabaster head is a representation of Alexander the Great. Alexander was believed to have stopped once at the temple at Taposiris Magna.

STATUE OF A ROYAL PERSON Right: This figure, found at Taposiris, shows a Ptolemaic royal standing in a pose commonly seen in ancient Egyptian sculpture.

"No grave upon the earth shall clip in it / A pair so famous."
— William Shakespeare, Antony and Cleopatra

THE LIFE OF CLEOPATRA

After Cleopatra and Mark Antony's doomed battle against Octavian at Actium, the Romans invaded Alexandria. When Cleopatra realized she would be taken prisoner, she packed her most treasured possessions into her mausoleum. Meanwhile, Antony had heard that Cleopatra had killed herself. In the ancient world, suicide was noble: As immortals, Antony and Cleopatra believed they would be reunited in the afterlife. Convinced the rumors were true, Antony took his own life. Cleopatra's servant Diomedes arrived as Antony lay dying and brought him to Cleopatra. Grief-stricken, Cleopatra returned to her palace and ended her life before Octavian could parade her through the streets of Rome as his prisoner. Despite Octavian's anger at being thwarted, he allowed Cleopatra and Antony to be buried side by side in royal fashion.

Cleopatra by Michelangelo Buonarroti, 1533.

WATER VESSEL Right: This bronze water vessel, found at Taposiris Magna, was most likely used by priests during religious rituals at the temple of Isis.

PART OF A STATUE Below: A fragmented sculpture of an unknown Ptolemaic woman bears resemblance to the goddess Isis.

PIECE OF A STATUE Some experts believe this fragment may depict the Roman general Mark Antony, who was buried with Cleopatra.

THE LEGEND

Cleopatra's Legacy

Cleopatra died, but she never disappeared. As queen of Egypt, she was already a celebrity in her own lifetime—one who carefully manipulated her public image. Worshipped as a goddess in Egypt, Cleopatra's immense wealth and fame made her an intriguing, exotic figure to the rest of the ancient world. Rather than fading over time, the legend of Cleopatra grew. She inspired great writers and artists. Few images of her remained, and most records of her life were written by her mortal enemies, the Romans. Freed by a lack of hard information, artists could invent and reinvent her. Today, the obsession with Cleopatra in literature, the arts, and popular culture is stronger than ever.

CLEOPATRA IN FILM Left: Vivien Leigh starred as the Egyptian queen in the 1945 Academy Award-nominated film *Caesar and Cleopatra*.

COIN Below: Contemporary coins depict Cleopatra as unattractive. But official portraits such as this were conventional images of royalty, not reliable lifelike representations. They aimed to convey power, authority, and family resemblances with her Greek ancestors, not beauty.

"Age cannot wither her, nor custom stale / Her infinite variety."
— William Shakespeare,
Antony and Cleopatra

CLEOPATRA IN ART Through the ages, actors, poets, artists, and writers have found inspiration in the legendary queen of Egypt.

ELIZABETH TAYLOR AS CLEOPATRA Above: This 1990 rendering, *Liz (Cleopatra)* by David Parrish, pays homage to the 1963 movie starring Elizabeth Taylor and Richard Burton.

CLEOPATRA IN MUSIC Right: The cover for the score of the 1923 operetta *Die Perlen der Cleopatra (Cleopatra's Pearls)* was written by Oscar Straus.

EARLY ARTWORK Opposite: *Portrait of Simonetta Vespucci,* painted by Piero di Cosimo around 1480, portrays the Italian noblewoman as Cleopatra with an asp around her neck—alluding to the way in which Cleopatra died.

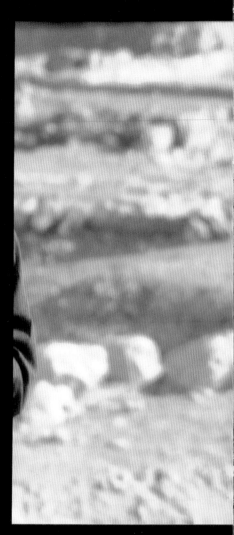

TAPOSIRIS MAGNA Zahi Hawass stands on site at Taposiris Magna, approximately thirty miles outside of Alexandria, where he is looking for Cleopatra's tomb.

LOOKING AHEAD

Preserving the Future

As the final pharaoh of Egypt, Cleopatra lived her life at the center of some of the ancient world's most dramatic events. She also ruled the hearts of two powerful Romans, Julius Caesar and Mark Antony. For the last two decades, marine archaeologist Franck Goddio and archaeologist Zahi Hawass have worked to uncover items from Cleopatra's palace, tomb, and the cities she knew. Today, as more details of her life unfold—and more artifacts are discovered—Cleopatra remains as compelling as ever. To help protect Cleopatra's legacy and to further educate young people about ancient Egypt, Zahi Hawass is raising funds by selling a replica of the hat he wears on archaeological expeditions. The hat includes a copy of his signature inside. All profits from the sale of the hat go to the Suzanne Mubarak Children's Museum in Cairo. The hat can be purchased in the museum store or online.

GIFT SHOP Above: The gift shop in the Cleopatra exhibition sells replicas of Zahi Hawass's hat, books on the famous queen, and other keepsakes.

HAWASS'S HAT Right: This hat is an exact replica of one that archaeologist Zahi Hawass has worn on several expeditions. All proceeds from the hat benefit the Suzanne Mubarak Children's Museum in Cairo.

"For now, we can only wait and see whether this place will reveal answers about Egypt's most mysterious queen and one of the most elusive characters in history—Cleopatra."

— Zahi Hawass

STELA At Heracleion, a diver shines a light on a stela from King Nectanebo I.

CLEOPATRA
· THE SEARCH FOR THE LAST QUEEN OF EGYPT ·

Exhibit Merchandising would like to thank Arts and Exhibitions International, an AEG Live Company, the producers of the exhibition, for its assistance in procuring many of the images and photographs used in this catalog.

ARTS and EXHIBITIONS INTERNATIONAL

ARTS AND EXHIBITIONS INTERNATIONAL, *an AEG Live Company*
JOHN NORMAN, *President, Executive Producer*
ANDRES NUMHAUSER, *Executive Vice President*
MICHAEL SAMPLINER, *Chief Operating Officer*
MARK LACH, *Senior Vice President*
BRYAN HARRIS, *Vice President, Sales and Marketing*
NATASHA BADGEROW, *Senior Project Manager*
CHANTELLE BLAYNEY, *Project Manager*
KRISTINA ROBBINS, *Project Manager*
JASON SIMMONS, *General Manager*
JEFF WYATT, *Vice President, Project Management*
LAURA CALLIARI, *Senior Director, Public Relations*
BRAD NUCCIO, *Vice President, Business Development*
ARBANA DOLLANI, *Assistant Project Manager*
KATIE LYNN BEACH, *Director of Ticket Operations*
JENNIFER LAROCK, *Manager of Ticket Operations*
CHRISTINA WRIGHT, *Project Manager*
BERNADETT SWARTHOUT, *Accounting*
MARCIA MARSHALL, *Accounts Payable*
JESSICA BAYNARD, *Staff Accountant*
JOLIE KASS, *Director of Exhibition Operations*
JACLYN PYATT, *General Manager*
MICHAEL PYATT, *Asst. General Manager*
GEMMA LEVETT, *General Manager*
BETH CRAWFORD, *Asst. General Manager*
RICHARD BRIGHT, *Production Manager*

Content, Design, and Installation
SHARON SIMPSON, SJS PROJECTS, INC., *Exhibition Writer*
TOM FRICKER, FRICKER STUDIO, *Exhibition Designer*
DAVID P. SILVERMAN, *Guest Curator*
DAVID DAILING, *Artifact Supervisor*
DAVID CARONE, *Registrar*
ALLAN SPRECHER, *Artifact Installation*
ATLANTIC PRODUCTIONS, *Media Production*
MARGARET B. STOGNER, BLUE BEAR FILMS, *Media Production*
DARRYL KINSON, *Media Production*
KENNETH L. GARRETT, *Photography*
DAVID MAUK, *Music Composition*

SAM REMBERT, *Lighting Production*
HEATHER WATSON, EILEEN HIRAIKE, HUNT DESIGN, *Graphic Design*
MOSS COMMUNICATIONS, *Scenic Fabric & Imagery Production*
CRUSH CREATIVE, *Graphic Production*
DESIGN ELECTRONICS, *Audio/Visual*
BENOSH PRODUCTIONS, *Display Production*
LEXINGTON STUDIOS, *Exhibition Production*

EXHIBIT MERCHANDISING LLC

Exhibit Merchandising is proud to be the exclusive retail partner for the Cleopatra Exhibition. Additionally, the company provides merchandising support for the traveling Tutankhamun and other exhibitions.

10145 Philipp Pkwy, Unit D
Streetsboro, OH 44241
www.ExhibitMerchandising.com
330-650-5570

CURTIS A. BECHDEL, *VP Operations*
CARL CARTER, *Director of Operations*
KAREN FORMANEK, *Executive Assistant*
COLLEEN NEWMAN, *Cleopatra Museum Store Manager*
BETHANY MIGLIORE, *Graphic Design*
JOSEPH POWELL, *Lead Carpenter*

Support Staff

LINDA CLIFFORD	VICTORIA JALM
JENNIE REED	GEORGE TISHMA
SAMANTHA PORCARO	TODD MARSHALL
PAT GREEN	AJ ELDESOUKY
KEVIN ARNOLD	DAWN BRATCHER
MARIE CULLINAN	

SPECIAL THANKS to Kristina Robbins, Chantelle Blayney, and Jason Simmons of AEI for their assistance in locating images and information.

 An Exhibition from
NATIONAL GEOGRAPHIC

 SPONSORED BY
HILTI FOUNDATION

NATIONAL GEOGRAPHIC SOCIETY
TERRY GARCIA, *Executive Vice President, Mission Programs*
SARAH LASKIN, *Vice President, Mission Programs*
KATHRYN KEANE, *Director, Traveling Exhibitions Development*
MIMI KOUMANELIS, *Vice President, Communications*
CYNDY BERDEL, *Communications*

FRANCK GODDIO, president of the Institut Européen d'Archéologie
Sous-Marine (IEASM) and director of the excavations, would like to
thank all those who have contributed to the success of the excavations
in Egypt:

In the Arab Republic of Egypt
FAROUK HOSNI, *Minister of Culture of Egypt*
ZAHI HAWASS, *Secretary General of the Supreme Council of Antiquities*

Supreme Council of Antiquities of Egypt
GENERAL SAMAH KCHTAB, *Financial Director*
SABRI ABD EL-AZIZ, *General Director of Egyptian Archaeology*
MOHAMED ABD EL-MAKSOUD, *Director of Egyptian Archaeology*
MOHAMED ABD EL-FATAH, *General Director of the Museums of Egypt*
MOHAMED ISMAÏL, *Director of the Foreign Archaeological Mission*
IBRAHIM A. DARWISH, *General Director of the Museums of Alexandria*

EGYPTIAN MUSEUM, *Cairo*
WAFAA EL-SADDIK, *Director, Egyptian Museum, Department of
    Exhibitions Abroad*
ALBERT GHALY, Egyptian Museum, *Department of Exhibitions Abroad*
LOTFI ABD EL-HAMID, *Egyptian Museum, Department of
    Exhibitions Abroad*

MARITIME MUSEUM, *Alexandria*
GRECO-ROMAN MUSEUM, *Alexandria*
NATIONAL MUSEUM, *Alexandria*
BIBLIOTHECA ALEXANDRINA
UNIVERSITY OF ALEXANDRIA

SPECIAL THANKS to the Egyptian Coast Guard and the Egyptian
Navy, responsible for the maritime area in which the mission has
taken place.

This project would not have been possible without the passionate
work of all the participants in the various missions in Egypt, the
collaboration and support of the Supreme Council of Antiquities, and
the knowledge and advice of the scientists who have supported us.

SPECIAL THANKS to the Hilti Foundation for its generous support
of the continuing work of IEASM and for its contributions to this
exhibition and the accompanying book.

www.franckgoddio.org

BECKON BOOKS

*Cleopatra: The Search for the Last Queen of Egypt (Official
Exhibition Guide)* was developed by Beckon Books in
cooperation with Exhibit Merchandising. Beckon Books
is an imprint of FRP Books, 2451 Atrium Way, Nashville,
Tennessee, 37214. Beckon publishes custom books for
cultural attractions, corporations, and non-profit
organizations.

CHRISTOPHER G. CAPEN, *President*
MONIKA STOUT, *Design/Production*
BETSY HOLT, *Editor*
www.beckonbooks.com
877-311-0155

FRP, Inc. is a wholly owned subsidiary of Southwestern/
Great American, Inc., Nashville, Tennessee.

ISBN: 978-1-935442-06-6
Printed in the United States of America
10 9 8 7 6 5 4 3 2 1

PHOTO CREDITS AND COPYRIGHTS:
Unless otherwise indicated, all images are © JackRamsdale.com.
Courtesy of AEI: 6a, 16a, 23a, 31a, 42a, 42b, 43
Art Resource, NY: 38a
Bildarchiv Preussischer Kulturbesitz/Art Resource, NY: 8f
Savina Croning: front cover art
De A Picture Library/Art Resource, NY: 8c
Kenneth Garrett: 8
Erich Lessing/Art Resource, NY: 8b
Réunion des Musées Nationaux/Art Resource, NY: 8g
Sandro Vannini: Page 8d, 8e
IEASM: 9a
Jérôme Delafosse, ©Franck Goddio/ Hilti Foundation: 27a
Christoph Gerigk, ©Franck Goddio/ Hilti Foundation: front
cover c and e, 3b, 6b, 7, 9b, 10, 11b, 15a, 15b, 15c, 16b, 19a, 19b, 20a,
20b, 20c, 20d, 23b, 23c, 24b, 24c, 25, 27b, 31a, 31b, 35c, 46, back
cover b and e